D0553011

Jon Balserak

Purchased 6/29/94 at Rock Creek Bookshop after the Saudi vs. Belgium world Cup game.

94/25

KT-365-251

REASON AND REVELATION IN THE MIDDLE AGES

by ETIENNE GILSON

Also published by Charles Scribner's Sons

THE SPIRIT OF MEDIAEVAL PHILOSOPHY

THE UNITY OF PHILOSOPHICAL EXPERIENCE

REASON AND REVELATION IN THE MIDDLE AGES

By

Etienne Gilson

CHARLES SCRIBNER'S SONS · NEW YORK

COPYRIGHT, 1938, BY
CHARLES SCRIBNER'S SONS
C-6.62[C]
Printed in the United States of America

All rights reserved. No part of this book may be reproduced in any form without the permission of Charles Scribner's Sons

To my friend

ALBERT G. A. BALZ

Corcoran Professor of Philosophy
in the University of
Virginia

Foreword

It is a pleasant duty, for visiting lecturers, to begin by expressing their gratitude to their hosts. In no case would I have forgotten to do it. But my indebtedness to the University of Virginia has far deeper roots than this occasion, the Richard Lectures for 1937. It was my privilege, eleven years ago, to begin my first visit to the United States by spending half a day in New York and nearly two months in Charlottesville. I say it was a privilege, because the memory of the days I have spent in this University has ever since remained with me, as a safeguard against the temptation, fatal to foreigners, to explore America from the top of the Empire State Building. To the friends and colleagues who then invited me, but no less to the students of the Summer School of 1926, who kindly helped me through a difficult task, I beg to renew today the expression of my lasting gratitude.

ETIENNE GILSON.

Contents

FOREWORD vii

I. THE PRIMACY OF FAITH 1

II. THE PRIMACY OF REASON 35

III. THE HARMONY OF REASON AND REVELATION 67

NOTES 101

INDEX 111

CHAPTER ONE

I

The Primacy of Faith

THE SUBJECT of these chapters not only recommends itself to us by its intrinsic merits, but it also provides an unusually favorable occasion to exercise that essential function of university teaching, the criticism of commonly received opinions. This criticism, which is obviously relevant in a positive science, is no less relevant in history. Now it is not unusual, in textbooks of general history, to distinguish three main periods in the development of Western thought. There first comes the age of Greek philosophy, the so-called "Greek miracle," a sort of Golden Age of human thought, that witnessed the quiet and undisturbed triumph of pure rational knowledge. Next come the Middle Ages, also called the Dark Ages, because from the rise of

Christianity to the dawn of the Renaissance, the normal use of natural reason was obscured by blind faith in the absolute truth of Christian Revelation. Philosophy then became a mere tool at the hands of unscrupulous theologians until at last, around the end of the fifteenth century, the joint effort of the humanists, of the scientists and of the religious reformers gave rise to the new era of purely positive and rational speculation in which we still find ourselves engaged.

What an historian of Greek philosophy can think of so simplified a view of his own field of studies, I am not prepared to say. Nor am I planning to discuss such views with regard to modern philosophy, but it is my intention, in these chapters, to test their truth value in so far as the Middle Ages are concerned. And I beg to make this quite clear, from the very beginning, that I am not at all planning to defend the Middle Ages against what is most certainly an unfair interpretation. I shall not even attempt to define and to maintain a new one. Of the Middle Ages as a whole, I have indeed no interpretation. But we can hope to achieve, if not a description of those seven centuries of abstract speculation, at least a sketch of the main spiritual families which were responsible for the copious philosophical and theological literature of the Middle Ages. I am too well aware of the fact that even so modest a result cannot be achieved without some violence done to the irreducible originality of the various medieval thinkers. We shall have sometimes to group together some men who would have taken no pleasure in finding themselves in the same class. It may nevertheless be hoped that our classification will prove as natural as classifications of human types can possibly be. At any rate, it should not be considered a waste of time to substitute for the usually received one a less conventional convention.

The first of those spiritual families, and the only one we will now attempt to characterize, was made up of those theologians according to whom Revelation had been given to men as a substitute for all other knowledge, including science, ethics and metaphysics. Ever since the very origin of Christianity up to our own days, there have always been such extremists in theology. Reduced to its essentials, their position is very simple; since God has spoken to us, it is no longer necessary for us to think. The only thing that matters for every one of us is to achieve his own salvation; now all that we need to know in order to achieve it is there, written down in the Holy Scriptures; let us therefore read the divine law, meditate upon it, live according to its precepts, and we shall stand in need of nothing else, not even of philosophy. I should rather say: particularly *not* of philosophy. In point of fact, we shall do infinitely better without philosophical knowledge than with it. Consider even the greatest among the Greek philosophers, including those whose teaching more or less resembled that of Christian Revelation, and you will find it everywhere at variance with the contents of Christian Revelation. Plato believed in an eternal transmigration of souls from their former bodies to other human, or even animal bodies. Aristotle denied Divine Providence and did not even believe in the personal immortality of the soul. The Stoics and the Epicureans were materialists. Even if we assume that what they claimed to know about God were true, what are we going to say about that which God Himself has revealed to us, and which they certainly did not know? Can man be saved unless he knows the fact of original sin, the Incarnation of Christ, the redemption of man through His death on the cross, and grace, and the Church with its sacraments? If such have been the errors and the shortcomings of the greatest among philosophical geniuses, their very blindness in matters of vital importance, there is no reason why true Christians should pay the slightest attention to what philosophers may have said on those questions. As Saint Paul himself once said: "Professing themselves to be wise, they become fools." (Rom. 1:22.) And again: "For seeing that in the wisdom of God the world by wisdom knew not God, it pleased God, by the foolishness of our preaching, to save them that believe. . . . the foolishness of God is wiser than men." (I Cor. 1:21, 25.) In short, since he who merely believes in the word of God knows more than the greatest philosophers have ever known concerning the only matters of vital importance, we should feel justified in saying that the simplest among Christians has a philosophy of his own, which is the only true philosophy, and whose name is: Revelation.*[1]

This absolute conviction in the self-sufficiency of Christian Revelation has always found decided supporters. We find it represented in all the significant periods of the history of Christian thought; its representatives are always there, but it becomes vocal chiefly during such times when philosophy is threatening to invade the field of Revelation. As early as the second century, when gnosticism became a real danger, Tertullian found forceful formulas to stress what he held to be an irreconcilable antagonism between Christianity and philosophy. The seventh chapter of his treatise *On prescription against heretics* is but a violent attack against what the Lord Himself called the "foolishness" of philosophy: "For philosophy it is which is the material of the world's wisdom, the rash interpreter of the nature and dispensation of God. Indeed heresies are themselves instigated by philosophy. The same subject matter is discussed over and over again by the heretics

*The footnotes, being almost entirely of a bibliographical nature, have been placed at the back of the book.

and the philosophers; the same arguments are involved. Whence comes evil? Why is it permitted? What is the origin of man? And in what way does he come? Besides the question which Valentius has very lately proposed—Whence comes God? Which he settles with the answer: From *enthymesis* and *ectroma.* Unhappy Aristotle! who invented for these men dialectics, the art of building up and pulling down, an art so far-fetched in its conjectures, so harsh in its arguments, so productive of contentions—embarrassing even to itself, retracting everything, and really treating of nothing!" Has not Saint Paul already warned us from such dangerous speculations, when he wrote to the Colossians, saying: "Beware lest any man cheat you by philosophy, and vain deceit; according to the tradition of men . . . and not according to Christ." (Col. 2:8.) Until at last, giving rein to his eloquent indignation, Tertullian exclaims: "What indeed has Athens to do with Jerusalem? What concord is there between the Academy and the Church? what between heretics and Christians? Our instruction comes from the porch of Solomon (Acts 3:5) who had himself taught that the Lord should be sought in simplicity of heart. (Wisd. 1:1.) Away with all attempts to produce a mottled Christianity of Stoic, Platonic and dialectic composition! We want no curious disputation after possessing Christ Jesus, no inquisition after enjoying the Gospel! With our faith, we desire no further belief. For this is our palmary faith, that there is nothing which we ought to believe besides."[2]

I have quoted Tertullian at some length, because of the very perfection with which he exemplifies that typical attitude. All its essential features are already there, and I do not think we could find a single one of these sentences that was not quoted again and again from the second century until the end of the Middle Ages, or even later. Let us call this family the Tertullian family, and I am sure you will never fail to identify its members when you meet them. In spite of their personal differences, the species itself is so easily recognizable! Emphasis laid upon three or four texts of Saint Paul, always the same, and exclusion of all his other statements about our natural knowledge of God, and the existence, nay, the binding force of a natural moral law; unqualified condemnation of Greek philosophy, as though no Greek philosopher had ever said anything true concerning the nature of God, of man and of our destiny; bitter hatred, and vicious attacks especially directed against Dialectics, as if it were possible even to condemn Dialectics without making use of it; the tracing back of heresies against religious dogmas to the pernicious influence of philosophical speculation upon theological knowledge; last, not the least, the crude statement of an absolute opposition between religious faith in the word of God and the use of natural reason in matters pertaining to Revelation; all those features, whose interrelation is obvious, help in defining the members of the Tertullian family and in perceiving what confers upon the group at least a loose unity of its own.

To limit ourselves to a small number of typical cases, let us recall the Greek writer Tatian, whose *Address to the Greeks* is but the violent protest of a Christian barbarian against the pride which the pagan Greeks were taking in their so-called civilized institutions. "What noble thing have you produced by your pursuit of philosophy?" Tatian asks. And after a long series of attacks against Plato and Aristotle, the Stoics and the Epicureans, we find him in full agreement with the conclusion of Tertullian, whom he had certainly not read: "Obeying the commands of God, and following the law of the Father of immortality, we reject everything which rests upon human opinion."[3] If we pass from the second to the twelfth century, in a time when the magnificent development of Logic could not but worry men of the Tertullian family, we find interesting specimens of this fierce theological species. The great Saint Bernard himself exhibited some of their traits. He probably had Peter Abelard in mind while he was writing his third *Sermon for the Feast of Pentecost.* At any rate, Bernard had obviously no use for those men who "called themselves philosophers," but, in his own opinion, "should rather be called the slaves of curiosity and pride." He did not want his brethren to belong to this school, but rather to the school of that supreme teacher to whom the feast of Pentecost is dedicated: the Holy Ghost. Because they had indeed attended

His divine school, each of them could say with the Psalmist (Ps. 119:99): *I have understood more than all my teachers.* And carried away by his admirable eloquence, Bernard suddenly exclaimed: "Wherefore, O my brother, dost thou make such a boast? Is it because . . . thou has understood or hast endeavored to understand the reasonings of Plato and the subtleties of Aristotle? God forbid! thou answerest. It is because I have sought Thy commandments, O Lord."[4] Saint Peter Damiani, with his much more vicious attacks on Dialectics, Grammar, and generally speaking all that which involved the slightest reliance upon the power of natural reason, would be a still more complete, though much less lovable instance of the same tendency.[5] In the thirteenth and fourteenth centuries, the passionate and, at times, savage controversy that raged, within the Franciscan Order, between its extremists—the so-called Spirituals, and the partisans of a well-conducted study of philosophy—had no other cause than the radical theologism of those Spirituals. The Franciscan poet Jacopone da Todo was a Spiritual, and he merely voiced their common feeling when he wrote, in one of his most famous poems: "Paris has destroyed Assise," and again:

> Plato and Socrates may contend
> And all the breath in their bodies spend,
> Arguing without an end—
> What's it all to me?
> Only a pure and simple mind
> Straight to heaven its way doth find;
> Greets the King—while far behind
> Lags the world's philosophy.[6]

The partisans of exclusive otherworldliness in the order of knowledge have been present wherever and whenever churchmen were interested in scientific and philosophical studies to the point of becoming actively engaged in the task of fostering their progress. The devil who visited Albertus Magnus in his cell, while the Saint was busy in solving some scientific problem, must have been a particularly clever unclean spirit, since he managed to appear in the garb of a Dominican Friar. And what was his message to the Saint? Simply that he was spending his time in occupations foreign to his profession, and should devote less time to science, but more to theology. Then, the old Chronicle goes on to say: "Albert, interiorly warned by the Divine Spirit of the impostor's design, contented himself with making the sign of the cross, and the phantom disappeared."[7] So much theological zeal in a devil was bound to look suspicious.

Had the Middle Ages produced men of this type only, the period would fully deserve the title of Dark Ages which it is commonly given. It would deserve the name not only from the point of view of science and of philosophy, but from that of theology as well. Fortunately, the history of Christian thought attests the existence of another spiritual family, much more enlightened than the first one, and whose untiring efforts to blend religious faith with rational speculations have achieved really important results. No less than those of the first group, the members of the second could find in the Bible texts to justify their own attitude. Not only had Saint Paul clearly stated that even pagans should be able to achieve a natural knowledge of the existence of God, "his eternal power also and divinity, so that they are inexcusable" (Rom. 1:20), but, in the first chapter of his Gospel, Saint John also had said that the Word of God "was the true light, which enlighteneth every man that cometh into this world." (John 1:9.) No wonder then that the greatest among the Greek Fathers of the Church —Justin Martyr, Clement of Alexandria, and Origen—built up theological doctrines in which the fundamental agreement of natural and revealed knowledge was everywhere either stated or presupposed. Yet, by far the most perfect representative of this group was, and is very likely to remain, a Latin Father—Saint Augustine. For the sake of brevity, and using the name as a mere practical label, let us call the representatives of this second tendency the Augustinian family. What were its essential characteristics?

We all remember the chapters of his *Confessions*, where Augustine relates how, after vainly trying to reach truth, and eventually faith, by means of reason alone, he had at last discovered that all the rational truth about God that had been taught by the philosophers could be grasped at once, pure of all errors, and enriched with many a more than philosophical truth by the simple act of faith of the most illiterate among the faithful. From that time on, Augustine was never to forget that the safest way to reach truth is not the one that starts from reason and then goes on from rational certitude to faith, but, on the contrary, the way whose starting point is faith and then goes on from Revelation to reason.

By reaching that unexpected conclusion, Augustine was opening a new era in the history of western thought. No Greek philosopher could have ever dreamt of making religious faith in some revealed truth the obligatory starting point of rational knowledge. In point of fact, Socrates, Plato, Aristotle, the Stoics and even the Epicureans, had always been busy in refining and rationally reinterpreting the crude myths of Greek paganism. By far the highest type of religious thought among the Ancients was that of their philosophers. With Saint Augustine, on the contrary, a new age was beginning, in which by far the highest type of philosophical thinking would be that of the theologians. True enough, even the faith of an Augustinian presupposes a certain exercise of natural reason. We cannot believe something, be it the word of God Himself, unless we find some sense in the formulas which we believe. And it can hardly be expected that we will believe in God's Revelation, unless we be given good reasons to think that such a Revelation has indeed taken place. As modern theologians would say, there are motives of credibility. Yet, when all is said, the most forceful reasons to believe that God has spoken cannot take us further than that belief itself. Now to believe that God has spoken, and that what God has said is true, is something essentially different from a rational comprehension of the truth which we hold by faith. We *believe* that it is true, but no Christian can hope to *know*, at least in this life, the truth which he believes. Yet, among those truths which he believes, the Christian finds the divine promise later to contemplate the God of his faith, and in that contemplation, to find eternal beatitude; hence, already in this life, his passionate effort to investigate the mysteries of Revelation by the natural light of reason. The result of such an effort is precisely what Augustine used to call *intellectus; understanding*, that is to say, some rational insight into the contents of Revelation, human reason groping its way towards the full light of the beatific vision.

Such is the ultimate meaning of Augustine's famous formula: "Understanding is the reward of faith. Therefore seek not to understand that thou mayest believe, but believe that thou mayest understand."[8] And again, in a longer but much more complete statement: "If to believe were not one thing and to understand another, and unless we had first to believe the great and divine thing which we desire to understand, the Prophet would have spoken idly when he said: 'Unless you believe, you shall not understand.' (Is. 7:9; secund. 70.) Our Lord Himself, too, by His words and deeds exhorted those whom He called to salvation, that they first believe. But afterwards, when He was talking of the gift which He would give to believers, He did not say, 'This is eternal life that you may *believe*,' but 'This is eternal life: that they may *know* Thee, the only true God, and Jesus Christ Whom Thou hast sent.' (John 17: 13.) Furthermore, He said to those who were already believers, 'Seek and you shall find.' (Matt.

7:7.) For what is believed unknown cannot be called found, nor is any one capable of finding God, unless he first believe that he will eventually find Him. . . . That which we seek on His exhortation, we shall find by His showing it to us, so far as it is possible to such as us to find this in this life . . . and we must surely believe that after this life this will be perceived and attained more clearly and more perfectly."[9]

It thus appears from Augustine's explicit statement, first that we are invited by Revelation itself to believe, that unless we believe we shall not understand; next that far from inviting us to do away with reason, the Gospel itself has promised to all those who seek truth in the revealed word the reward of understanding. Whence it follows that instead of entailing its ultimate rejection the doctrine of Saint Augustine was achieving a transfiguration of the Greek ideal of philosophical wisdom. What the greatest among the Pagans, such as Plato and Plotinus, had always been hoping for, was now at hand. For the Greek philosophers had passionately loved wisdom, but grasp it they could not; and there it now was, offered by God Himself to all men as a means of salvation by faith, and, to the philosophers, as an unerring guide towards rational understanding.

From the fourth century after Christ till our own days, there have always been men to uphold, or to revive, the Augustinian ideal of Christian Wisdom. All the members of the Augustinian family resemble one another by their common acceptance of the fundamental principle: unless you believe, you shall not understand. Moreover, being Christians, all of them agree that the only conceivable faith is faith in Christian Revelation. Yet, despite their unmistakable family air, the members of that remarkably united family have always been conspicuous by their personal originality. You cannot fail to know an Augustinian when you meet one in history, but it is not an easy thing to guess what he is going to say. The reason for it is, that while all the members of the family hold the same faith, in whatever places and times they happen to live, not all of them use their understanding in the same way. The faith upheld by Augustine in the fourth century was substantially the same one as that of Saint

Anselm in the eleventh century, of Saint Bonaventura in the thirteenth, of Malebranche in the seventeenth, and of Gioberti in the nineteenth, but while their common set of beliefs exhibits this remarkable stability, the received views on the proper use of human reason were constantly changing around them. In short, all the Augustinians agree that unless we believe, we shall not understand; and all of them agree as to what we should believe, but they do not always agree as to what it is to understand.

Hence the remarkable aptness of the Augustinian family to stand the test of time. The most drastic intellectual revolutions merely provide Augustinians with a new occasion to manifest their permanent vitality. To Saint Augustine himself, the perfect type of rational knowledge was the philosophy of Plato, as revised and brought up to date by Plotinus. Consequently, given his own idea of what rational knowledge is, the whole philosophical activity of Saint Augustine had to be a rational interpretation of the Christian Revelation, in terms of platonic philosophy. As Saint Thomas Aquinas was later going to say: Augustine has followed in the wake of the Platonists as far as he could possibly go with them.[10] The most exacting historical research can but confirm Thomas' statement. The Augustinian conceptions of man, of the relations of soul and body, of sense knowledge and of intellectual knowledge, are obviously Christian reinterpretations of the corresponding notions in both Plato and Plotinus. By attempting such reinterpretations from a Christian point of view, Augustine was condemned to being original. In all his works, the platonic frame is, so to speak, bursting under the internal pressure of its Christian contents. That was unavoidable in most cases, but quite particularly when Augustine had to turn the plotinian Logos into the Word of Saint John, or to transmute the platonic doctrine of reminiscence into a Christian doctrine of the divine illumination.[11] Yet, when all is said, it still must be maintained that the net result of Augustine's philosophical speculation was to achieve a platonic understanding of the Christian Revelation.

Let us now consider another thinker of the same type, Saint Anselm of Canterbury. As he himself repeatedly said, his only ambition was to restate what his master Augustine had already stated. And that is exactly what he did.[12] Moreover, Anselm was so fully convinced of the validity of Augustine's method that its most perfect definitions are to be looked for in the writings of Anselm rather than in those of Augustine. Anselm, not Augustine, is responsible for the famous formula: *credo ut intelligam:* "I do not endeavor, O Lord, to penetrate thy sublimity for in no wise do I compare my understanding with that; but I long to understand in some degree thy truth, which my heart believes and loves. For I do not seek to understand that I may believe, but I believe in order to understand. For this also I believe, that unless I believed, I should not understand."[13] But Anselm wrote his treatises during the last years of the eleventh century; he had not gone through the ordeal of Augustine's conversion and was not indebted to Plato, nor to Plotinus, for his discovery of what intellectual knowledge actually is. To him, as to all his contemporaries, rational knowledge was logical knowledge. In his mind, and in the mind of his disciples, a rational demonstration was a dialectical demonstration made up of faultlessly knitted syllogisms. In short, in Anselm's own times, the standard science was Logic. Under such circumstances, the same endeavor, to achieve a rational understanding of Christian faith, was bound to result in a new translation of Christian beliefs into terms of logical demonstration.

Why, for instance, did Anselm ever think of what we now call his "ontological proof" of the existence of God? Because a purely logical demonstration of the existence of God had to be wholly *a priori*, that is, deduced from the sole concept of God, without resorting to empirical knowledge. Whatever its ultimate metaphysical implications may be, the so-called ontological argument is an essentially dialectical deduction of the existence of God, whose internal necessity is that of the principle of contradiction. God is that than which nothing greater can be conceived; if it can be shown that it is contradictory to think of the greatest conceivable being as non-existing, God's existence will have been fully demonstrated. And there will be no use in arguing, with Gaunilo and Saint Thomas, that what such a proof verifies is merely this, that it is impossible for us to think of

God as not existing; for indeed a logician does not need more than that to get full rational satisfaction. As a Christian, Anselm believes there is a God; as a logician, he concludes that the notion of a non-existing God is a self-contradictory notion; since he can neither believe that there is no God, nor conceive it, there follows that God exists. By means of Logic alone, Anselm has achieved a rational understanding of Christian faith—the same faith as that of Augustine, but a different understanding.

Once a Christian thinker gets to this point, nothing could prevent him from applying the same method to each of the Christian dogmas. And indeed Anselm of Canterbury, as well as his immediate disciples, remain famous in the history of theology for their recklessness in giving rational demonstrations of all revealed truths. To limit ourselves to Anselm himself, we find him proving, by conclusive dialectical arguments, not only the Trinity of the Divine Persons, as he did in both his *Monologium* and his *Proslogium*, but even the very Incarnation of Christ, including all its essential modalities, as he did in his *Cur Deus homo.*

As he himself says in his Preface, the first part of that treatise, "leaving Christ out of view, as if nothing had ever been known of Him, proves, by necessary reasons, the impossibility that any man should be saved without Him. Again, in the second book, likewise as if nothing were known of Christ, it is moreover shown as no less patent rational truth, that human nature was ordained for that purpose, *viz.* that some time the whole man should enjoy a happy immortality, both in body and in soul; and that it was necessary that this design for which man was made should be fulfilled; but that it could not be fulfilled unless God became man, so that all things which we hold with regard to Christ had necessarily to take place."[14] This bold ambition to procure necessary reasons for the revealed dogmas had never entered the mind of Saint Augustine; but it was bound to follow from a merely dialectical treatment of Christian faith. The original character of the doctrine of Saint Anselm, and the peculiar aspect which it still offers to the investigating historian, have no other source and can be accounted for in no other way.

Let us now jump over the twelfth century and

the Augustinian landscape will once more appear to us as both constant in its general outline, and different in its population. The same Christian Revelation is still there, and there still are men whose ambition it is to understand it. For what is wisdom indeed, if not the rational understanding of faith? But again, what is it to understand? To such a man as Roger Bacon, who was writing in the second half of the thirteenth century, there was no doubt that Logic is a necessary instrument for anyone who wishes to acquire knowledge; but at the same time, Bacon was of the opinion that his contemporaries were overrating its value. His own contribution to the epistemology of the Middle Ages was to be a stronger emphasis upon two rational methods much too neglected in the thirteenth-century universities: mathematical demonstration and experimental investigation. Such had been his main discovery and it is enough to open any one of his later works in order to find it there, under the form of either its statement or some one of its many applications.

Mathematics, Bacon says, is superior to all the other sciences, at least in this, that "in mathematics we are able to arrive at the full truth without error, and at a certainty of all points involved without doubt. . . . But in other sciences, the assistance of mathematics being excluded, there are so many doubts, so many opinions on the part of man, that these sciences cannot be unfolded . . . ; for in these sciences there are from nature no processes of drawing figures and of reckonings, by which all things must be proved true. And therefore in mathematics alone is there certainty without doubt."[15] If a man thus minded happens to be, at the same time, not only a Christian, and a priest, and a Grey Friar, but a member of the Augustinian family, we can be sure that he will not be slow in using mathematics as a means towards the highest of his intellectual ends: achieving some understanding of Christian Revelation. Hence, in the *Opus majus* of Roger Bacon, his curious attempts at representing and expressing, by means of numbers and of geometrical figures, the mysteries of grace and predestination, the relationship between the unity of God and the Trinity of the Divine Persons, the necessarily low proportion of the just ones as compared with the number of the sinners and many other religious teachings of unequal importance.[16] But experimental science is still much more important than mathematics in the eyes of Roger Bacon; for it is true that mathematical demonstrations are binding, but they can do no more than convince us of the truth, they do not show it. Experiments make us see it, and such is the reason why even mathematics must sometimes resort to experimental demonstrations. Why not then add internal experiment to the external one? Mysticism will thus become an experimental knowledge of the revealed truth, nay, of all truth whatsoever, for it is a clear thing that he who has had diligent training in the use of the spiritual senses will be able "to assure himself and others not only in regard to things spiritual, but also in regard to all human sciences." To Bacon all knowledge is but a particular case of a universal revelation.[17]

Bacon was not to be the last known variety of the Augustinian species. Ramon Lull, who died in 1315, had also discovered a new way of proving truth, which he described at great length in his *Ars magna*, that is, his *Art of proving truth*. By combining together various symbols inscribed on concentric circles, Lull hoped to deduce the whole body of human knowledge in an almost mechanical way.[18] The only trouble with his complicated machine is that his disciples have never been able to agree as to the correct way of using it. But Lull himself could use it, and he applied its principles in another of his works, the *Book of Demonstrations,* where we still can find his demonstrations of the most hidden mysteries, including the Incarnation and the Trinity. To extract from his symbolic logic necessary and incontrovertible arguments in favor of the revealed truth, was his own way to achieve its understanding. True enough the only knowledge that is required from man for his salvation is faith; but as Understanding says in Lull's *Dialogue between Faith and Understanding:* "Those who *can* understand, *should* understand."[19] A perfect motto indeed for the whole Augustinian and Anselm tradition.

Even the most obstinate writer has to stop somewhere; let us therefore take leave of those medieval theologians, but not without stressing the grave difficulties that arise from a thus understood Christian Wisdom. These difficulties do not flow from any internal inconsistency to be found in its notion, but rather from the conditions required for its exercise. The combination of religious holiness with speculative genius always remains an open possibility, and every time it materializes, Christian Wisdom is at hand. To such men as Saint Anselm and Saint Augustine, religious faith is there, objectively defined in its contents by Revelation, as a reality wholly independent from their own personal preferences. In Malebranche's striking formula, religious dogmas are their "experiments" in matters of philosophy. Just as scientists accept observable facts as the very stuff which they have to understand, those religious geniuses accept the data of Revelation as the given facts which they have to understand. Yet, possible as it is, the happy combination of so widely different gifts must needs be rare. What more usually happens is, that instead of using science and philosophy to gain some insight into the rational meaning of Revelation, second-rate thinkers will use Revelation as a substitute for rational knowledge, not without causing serious damage to both Revelation and Reason. The net result of such mistakes always is, first, to render a truly natural knowledge impossible, and next to substitute for faith in the word of God a more or less rational assent to the conclusions of pseudo-demonstrations. Thus confronted with a wisdom of Christians, elaborated by Christians and for the exclusive benefit of Christians, unbelievers find themselves in a rather awkward position. They do not believe, hence they have nothing to understand. The only way out of such a situation is for them to pit against theology a purely philosophical wisdom, exclusively based upon the principles of natural reason and independent of religious revelation. By whom that ideal of a purely philosophical wisdom was upheld in the Middle Ages is the problem which the next chapter will take into consideration.

CHAPTER TWO

II

The Primacy of Reason

THE ORIGINS of modern rationalism are commonly traced back to the intellectual revolution which took place early in Italy, when such men as Galileo made their first scientific discoveries. And I am very far from saying that there is nothing true in that assertion. Some aspects at least of modern rationalism would not be what they are, and they are among the most significant ones, without the scientific Renaissance of the sixteenth century. The fact remains, however, that there has been another rationalism, much older than that of the Renaissance, and wholly unrelated to any scientific discovery. It was a purely philosophical rationalism, born in Spain, in the mind of an Arabian philosopher, as a conscious reaction against the theologism of the Arabian divines. The author of that reaction was Ibn Rochd, better known to us under the latinized form of his name: Averroës. When Averroës died, in 1198, he bequeathed to his successors the ideal of a purely rational philosophy, an ideal whose influence was to be such that, by it, the evolution even of Christian philosophy was to be deeply modified.

The rise of what we now call Averroism would remain a mystery if we did not know that, ever since the ninth century, many theological dialecticians had been working at establishing some conciliation between philosophical knowledge and Islamic faith. Those men had found themselves in just the same situation as the Fathers of the Church and the first scholastic theologians. On the one hand, they had at their disposal translations of the writings of Aristotle, plus a compilation known as *The Theology of Aristotle*, though it was but a collection of texts chiefly borrowed from the *Enneads* of Plotinus. On the other hand, they had their own revealed book, the Koran, and the problem for them was how to think as Aristotle if we believe as Mohammed.

The greatest among the predecessors of Averroës, Ibn Sina (Avicenna), had succeeded in solving that difficult problem by building up a philosophy whose crowning part was a natural theology, thus leaving a door open to the supernatural light of Revelation. What Avicenna really thought of the rational value of religious beliefs is not quite clear. If, as there are good reasons to believe, he did not make much of them, he at least was clever enough never to entangle himself in serious theological difficulties. And yet, the man who was, and remains even in our own days, the greatest theologian in Islam, Gazali, was not slow in noticing a serious divergence between the authentic teachings of the Koran and the conclusions of Avicenna. After summing up the main theses of Avicenna, he refuted them in his *Destruction of the Philosophers*, and endeavored to prove, by rational demonstrations, the fundamental articles of the Moslem creed.

It is typical of Averroës that he took up the challenge of Gazali, and, against his theological *Destruction of the Philosophers*, wrote a *Destruction of the Destruction*. To Averroës, the absolute truth was not to be found in any sort of Revelation, but in the writings of Aristotle, which he never tired of commenting on and annotating. When Aristotle had said something, reason itself had spoken, and there was nothing more to say about it. What then should we do, in those many cases where the conclusions of Aristotle seem to contradict the religious beliefs of the community? The bitter hatred of the Moslem divines, and their persecution against him, would not allow Averroës to ignore the question. He dealt with it in his treatise: *The Agreement of Religion and Philosophy*, a landmark in the history of western civilization.

The very title of this treatise is a safe indication that Averroës had no desire to hurt the feelings of the theologians. It must even be said that Averroës was really hoping to convince the theologians, that some sort of agreement between religious faith and philosophical reason was not an absolute impossibility. He certainly was of the opinion that no conflicts should arise between a faith which keeps its own place and a philosophy which is intelligent enough to realize the specific function of religion. The only problem is, what is that place and what is that function?

Averroës opens his discussion of the problem by

observing, that far from condemning the use of philosophical speculation, Revelation itself positively prescribes it. It is an imperative injunction of the religious law, that men should study the nature of things, that they may raise their minds to the knowledge of their common maker. But is not that also the proper business of philosophy? And if it is, does not Revelation itself make it a duty for us to philosophize? Now, no man can be asked to create philosophy out of nothing. Metaphysics is a very old science, which has already been cultivated for several centuries, especially by the Greeks. Consequently, Revelation cannot prescribe the study of philosophy without enjoining at the same time the study of Greek philosophy. Nor is that all. The Divine Law explicitly makes obligatory the observation and interpretation of nature by reason, so that we may infer God from His creation. But an inference is a definite mode of reasoning, and nobody can use it properly unless he knows first what are the various kinds of dialectical arguments and in what way the necessary conclusions of reason differ from the purely dialectical ones. In short, a man cannot possibly reason without first knowing what is reasoning and what is not reasoning, that is, without first knowing logic. Let us therefore quietly conclude that according to the very letter of the revealed Law, the philosopher is the only man who fulfils his religious duties and strictly obeys the prescriptions of Revelation.[1]

At this point, however, there arises a rather puzzling question. Were it true that the divine law enjoins us to seek God by the rational methods of philosophy, why should there be a supernatural revelation? In order to solve that problem, Averroës resorted to the Aristotelian distinction between the three main classes of arguments: the rhetorical, the dialectical and the necessary ones, and he suggested that all men be distributed among three corresponding classes: those who are apt to be persuaded by clever speech only, those that are more particularly open to dialectical probabilities, and those whom nothing can satisfy but the necessary demonstrations of the mathematicians and of the metaphysicians. Common people make up the whole population of the first class, which is by far the more crowded one. Such men are led by imagination rather than by reason, and the only people that are able to convince them are eloquent speakers who know how to stir their feelings by appropriate arguments. All good preachers know how to do it. You will not civilize a tribe of Bedouins by teaching them metaphysics. If you want them not to kill, not to plunder and not to drink, the only thing for you to do is to appeal to their imagination. Tell them, for instance, that there is another world, where the good ones will enjoy eternal fleshly pleasures, while the evil ones will undergo eternal bodily punishments. The question whether that is true or not is secondary in importance. The real question is, is it true that all men should master their passions? We know it is, and for very solid philosophical reasons. If that is true, all men should be persuaded to do it; but nobody can be convinced by reasons which he cannot understand, and that is the exact spot where the necessity of religion appears in full: religion and Revelation are nothing but philosophical truth made acceptable to men whose imagination is stronger than their reason.

Not so with the second class of men, that of the

dialectically minded ones. Materially speaking, they believe just the same things as the rank and file of the faithful, but they do not believe them in the same way. In order to convince such men it is not enough to appeal to their imagination and to stir their emotions; they cannot be brought to believe unless what they are asked to believe be made at least believable in the light of natural reason. In the first place, such men want to make sure that nothing of what is taught by Revelation is at variance with verified scientific knowledge. In the second place, they want to be given good reasons why they should believe this rather than that. Fortunately, nothing is easier for us than to find reasons in favor of what we already believe. Such precisely is the proper function of theology and of the theologians, not indeed to demonstrate the truth of Revelation for faith would no longer be faith if it could be rationally proven; but to find out some dialectical justifications whereby Revelation will appear as at least rationally probable, and even as more probable than its contrary. There is no reason in the world why such a thing should not be done. As a matter of fact, theology has its own function to fulfil, for if men of that type were forbidden to clothe their beliefs in a more or less philosophical garb, they would soon cease to believe, and not being able to grasp real demonstrations, they would be left without either faith or philosophy. In short, such men would have no principles to live by. Yet, true philosophers cannot adopt such an attitude. Nothing short of necessary rational demonstrations will quench their thirst for knowledge. The exceedingly small number of thus minded men makes up the third and highest class of human minds; but while enjoying their aristocratic privilege, such men should also be careful to discern and to respect the solid nucleus of truth which lies hidden behind the fancies of simple faith as well as behind the dialectical probabilities of the theologians. For instance, it is not true that the world has been created out of nothing by a superworkman of some sort, as the God of common faith is; philosophers will never accept that; yet they do know that the world is hanging from a first cause in both its existence and its intelligibility. Likewise, it is simply not true that the first cause has created the world in time; not a single one of the many arguments whereby the theologians have sought to prove that the world has had a beginning in time is of any value and no true philosopher will ever believe it; yet philosophers know by necessary demonstration that the first cause is eternally moving the world and necessarily begetting all that which is in virtue of its infinite fecundity. It can therefore be said, that these three different approaches to the same truth ultimately agree. What the mob are holding as true by faith and what the theologians are expressing in terms of dialectical probability, is nothing but philosophical truth itself, adapted to the use of those lower classes of minds. Faith is the only possible approach to rational truth for men of imagination; theology is the next best thing to metaphysics for a merely dialectical mind; but philosophy itself is absolute truth, as established by the demonstrations of pure reason.[2]

Should all sensible men accept those conclusions, the perpetual strife that is raging between simple believers, theologians and philosophers would either come to an end or, at least, it would boil down to something like the common frictions of social life. No tragic conflicts between philosophers and theologians would ever arise, were it not for the harmful inclination of so many amongst us to mind somebody else's business. What is the matter with the faithful is not that they are simple believers, but rather that they will play at being theologians; and theologians themselves are all right *qua* theologians, but you won't stop them playing at being philosophers; and, to be quite fair, let us add that philosophers are unimpeachable so long as they leave faith and theology alone, but they won't do it. Yet they ought to, and plain common sense should warn them off such grounds. In point of fact, thoughtful metaphysicians never find themselves in conflict with any conceivable revelation. Most of the time, their rational speculation will lead them to conclusions of which Revelation says nothing; in such cases, there can be no opposition between reason and Revelation. In the other cases, that is, when Revelation and reason have to deal with the same problems, they are bound either to agree or to disagree. Assuming that they do agree, there is no conflict.

And assuming they disagree? Then the philosopher should not expect the faithful and the theologians to see his point; even though they would, they simply could not do it. It is up to him to make allowance for their own difficulties and to respect, in both their beliefs and their dogmas, the nucleus of philosophical truth that lies there. Let the philosophers do this, and there will never be any strife between reason and Revelation.[3]

This is how it may be. But with all due respect to the perfect sincerity of Averroës' own intentions, I fail to see how he could possibly hope to placate the theologians by advocating such a policy. I am not quite sure that philosophers could be easily persuaded to dismiss religion as being but a crude approach to philosophy, but if a philosopher starts teaching that there should be a religion for the mob,[4] unless the man be a fool, he cannot seriously hope to get away with it. There is little consolation for theologians, in hearing it said that Revelation is the next best thing to philosophy, and that his own definition finally is: a man who is not able to be a philosopher. As we all know from bitter experience, some philosophers do preach, but all preachers love to demonstrate. Averroës himself knew it so well, that after explaining to his fellow philosophers the whole truth about their superiority, he strongly advised them to keep that truth to themselves. Nay, he even advised them to keep philosophy to themselves, and never either to preach it to the mob or to fight for it against the theologians. The happy few whom God has endowed with a philosophical mind should content themselves with a solitary possession of rational truth. Let therefore philosophers discuss such matters among themselves; let them write down their conclusions in learned books, which their technical character will protect against the curiosity of the crowd; but don't let them disturb the peace of simple minds with demonstrations that are above them. Thus understood, philosophy becomes an esoteric and truly secret science, so much so that Averroës wondered if it were not a wise move officially to forbid the public use of philosophical books. In point of fact, nothing wiser could be conceived by a man whose main intention it was to establish a lasting peace between philosophers and theologians.[5]

The doctrinal position of Averroës was a very complex one and there is more in it than meets the eye. At first sight, it looks like a vicious attack against religion, and there is no denying that, from the point of view of the theologians it cannot bear any other interpretation. In the mind of Averroës himself however, things were far from being so simple. As most of the philosophers, he wanted social order, that he himself might philosophize in peace, and he knew full well that men could not possibly be civilized by merely being taught some abstract code of social ethics. In other words, Averroës did not consider religion as merely a rough approximation to philosophic truth. It was for him much more. It had a definite social function that could not be fulfilled by anything else, not even philosophy. Such is the exact meaning of the texts where he praises the Koran as a truly "miraculous" book. I see no reason not to take that word seriously. The more convinced Averroës was of the absolute superiority of philosophical knowledge, the more baffling must have been to him the existence of such a book, a book both wholly unphilosophical and much more effective than philosophy itself in raising barbarians to the level of morality. In order to account for that miracle, Averroës had finally to make room in his doctrine for the fact that there are Prophets. Prophets alone can perform miracles; but there are miracles of deeds, as for instance the dividing of the sea, which do not conclusively prove the prophecy of any one, and there are miracles of knowledge, which are the only conclusive proof of it. The existence of Prophets is an empirical fact, just as easily observable as that of traders or of physicians. They have no proofs of the existence of God, yet they know there is one, and when they say it, everybody believes it. They never ask themselves whether man has a soul or not. They know it. Moreover, as soon as they start preaching that man has indeed a soul, and that man's happiness ultimately hangs on his respect for such virtues as justice and charity, the wildest barbarians begin to listen, and behold something like real civilization actually sets in. To this you may object: granted that the Prophets accomplished so much, it remains a fact that what they say is not complete and absolute truth. But your very objection shows how miraculous were the accomplishments of the Prophets. Had he happened to live in such times, a philosopher would have demonstrated the whole and absolute truth, and nobody would have listened to it. In point of fact, nobody does even in our own times. Because he is divinely inspired, on the contrary, a true Prophet, as Moses, Jesus Christ or Mohammed, knows exactly both what quantity of truth the common people can take in, and how to catch the ear of so restive an audience. As the Koran itself says (19:47): "Verily, if men and angels were purposely assembled, that they might produce a book like this Koran, they could not produce one like it." And the Koran is right, for nothing short of a divine inspiration could have produced it.[6]

As you can see, there is a long cry from the historical Averroës and the legendary author of the pamphlet later on circulated under his name: *The Three Impostors.* Far from considering Moses, Jesus and Mohammed as three cunning deceivers, he always respected them as three messengers of God unto mankind. But even that was not enough to placate theologians; what they wanted him to say was that the word of God is above any human word, be it that of the greatest philosophers themselves. Now Averroës had always maintained that philosophical truth was absolute truth, the Koran and its theological interpretations being nothing more to him than popular approaches to pure philosophy. No wonder then that he had to undergo severe persecutions. He died in Morocco, an exile from his native Spain, in the year 1198.

Difficult to maintain in a Moslem civilization, the position of Averroës was a strictly impossible one for his Latin disciples in the thirteenth century. First of all, they do not seem to have known the particular treatise which he had devoted to a detailed study of that problem. Next, those men who were acquainted with his commentaries upon Aristotle, and who received his conclusions as true, could not possibly teach them as an expression of the absolute truth. Not only because they were Christians, and all of them clerics, that is, churchmen, was this the case, but also because most of them were teaching in the thirteenth-century University of Paris, a clerical institution directly controlled by ecclesiastical authorities. A professor of philosophy could not well be allowed to teach as true in the Faculty of Arts of that University, the very reverse of what his colleagues were teaching as true in the Faculty of Theology of the same University. In a Church Institution, the only absolute truth had to be theological truth. Such being the case, the problem of knowing whether or not such men were acquainted with Averroës' own treatment of the question is secondary in importance. Even knowing his complete answer to the problem, they could not have made public use of it. Hence their effort to work out such a position on the question as would prove acceptable from the point of view of the Church. In consequence of this, there was the rise of a new spiritual family: the Latin Averroists.

Among the many members of that family, I beg to distinguish a first variety, which I cannot help considering as entitled to our sincere sympathy. For indeed those poor people found themselves in sore straits. On the one side, they were good Christians and sincere believers. To them, it was beyond a doubt that Christian Revelation was, not only the truth, but the ultimate, supreme and absolute truth. This reason in itself was sufficient to make it impossible for them to be Averroists in identically the same way as Averroës himself. On the other side, and this time as philosophers, this group failed to see how any one of Averroës' philosophical doctrines could be refuted. What were they to do in the many instances where their faith and their reason were at odds? For instance, their philosophy proved by necessary reasons that the world is eternal, perpetually moved by a self-thinking thought or mind, ruled from above by an intelligible necessity wholly indifferent to the destinies of individuals as such. In point of fact, the God of the Averroists does not even know that there are individuals, he knows only himself and that which is involved in his own necessity. Thus, knowing the human species, he is in no wise aware of the existence of those fleeting things, the individuals by which the eternal species is represented. Besides, as individuals, men have no intellect of their own; they do not think, they are merely thought into from above by a separate intellect, the same for the whole of mankind. Having no personal intellect, men can have no personal immortality, nor therefore can they hope for future rewards or fear eternal punishments in another life. Yet, at the same time when their reason was binding them to accept those conclusions, as philosophers, their faith was binding them to believe, as Christians, that the world has been freely created in time, by a God whose fatherly providence takes care of even the smallest among His Creatures; and if God so cares for every sparrow, what shall we say of man, who is of more value than many sparrows? Is not each of us endowed with a personal intellect of his own, responsible for each one of his thoughts as well as of his acts, and destined to live an immortal life of blessedness or of misery according to his own individual merits? In short, theology and philosophy were leading these men to conclusions that could neither be denied nor reconciled.

In order to free themselves from those contradictions, some among the Masters of Arts of the Parisian Faculty of Arts chose to declare that, having been appointed to teach philosophy, and nothing else, they would stick to their own job, which was to state the conclusions of philosophy such as necessarily follow from the principles of natural reason. True enough, their conclusions did not always agree with those of theology, but such was philosophy and they could not help it. Besides, it should be kept in mind that these professors would never tell their students, nor even think among themselves, that the conclusions of philosophy were true. They would say only this, that such conclusions were necessary from the point of view of natural reason; but what is human reason as compared with the wisdom and power of an infinite God? For instance, the very notion of a creation in time is a philosophical absurdity, but if we believe in God Almighty, why should not we also believe that, for such a God to create the world in time was not an impossibility? The same thing could be said everywhere. The conclusions of philosophy are at variance with the teaching of Revelation; let us therefore hold them as the *necessary* results of philosophical speculation, but, as Christians, let us believe that what Revelation says on such matters is *true;* thus, no contradiction will ever arise between philosophy and theology, or between Revelation and reason.

The doctrine of this first group of Latin Averroists is commonly called: the doctrine of the twofold truth.[7] Philosophically justified as I think it is, such a designation is not an historically correct one. Not a single one among those men would have ever admitted that two sets of conclusions, the one in philosophy, the other in theology, could be, at one and the same time, both absolutely contradictory and absolutely true. There still are many medieval writings to be discovered, but with due reservation as to what could be found to the contrary in one of them, I can say that such a position was a most unlikely one, and that I have not yet been able to find a single medieval philosopher professing the doctrine of the twofold truth. Their actual position was a much less patently contradictory and a much less unthinkable one. As so many men who cannot reconcile their reason with their faith, and yet want them both, the Averroists were keeping both philosophy and Revelation, with a watertight separation between them. Why should not a man feel sure that Averroës cannot be refuted, and yet believe that the most necessary reasons fall short of the infinite wisdom of an all-powerful God? I would not say that it is a logically safe position, nor a philosophically brilliant one, but the combination of blind fideism in theology with scepticism in philosophy is by no means an uncommon phenomenon in the history of human thought. I seem to hear one of those divided minds saying to himself: here is all that philosophy can say about God, man and human destiny; it is not much; yet that at least is conclusively proven and I cannot make philosophy say anything else. Were we living in a non-Christian world, such conclusions would not be merely necessary, they would also be truth. But God has spoken. We now know that what appears as necessary in the light of a finite reason is not necessarily true. Let us therefore take philosophy for what it is: the knowledge of what man would hold as true, if absolute truth had not been given to him by the divine Revelation. There have been men of that type in the thirteenth-century University of Paris; to the best of my knowledge, there is no reason whatever to suppose that Siger of Brabant and Boethius of Dacia for instance, both of them Averroists in philosophy, were not also perfectly sincere in their religious faith. Such, at least, was the personal conviction of Dante concerning Siger, for had he entertained the least suspicion about the sincerity of Siger's faith, he would not have put him in the fourth heaven of the Sun, together with Albertus Magnus and Thomas Aquinas.[8]

Besides that first group of Latin Averroists, there was another one, whose members were equally convinced that the philosophy of Averroës was the absolute truth, but felt no difficulty in reconciling it with their religious beliefs, because they had none. It is often said, and not without good reasons, that the civilization of the Middle Ages was an essentially religious one. Yet, even in the times of the Cathedrals and of the Crusades, not everybody was a saint; it would not even be correct to suppose that everybody was orthodox, and there are safe indications that confirmed unbelievers could be met on the streets of Paris and of Padua around the end of the thirteenth century. When such men were at the same time philosophers, the deism of Averroës was their natural philosophy. As to Revelation, they would profess, at least in words, absolute respect for its teachings, but none of them would ever miss an opportunity to demonstrate by necessary reasons the very reverse of what they were supposed to believe. Seen from without, the members of this second group were saying identically the same things as the members of the first one, but their tone was different and, cautious as they had to be, they usually found the way to make themselves understood.

One of the best specimens of that variety was undoubtedly the French philosopher John of Jaudun, better known to historians as the associate of Marsiglio di Padoa in his campaign against the temporal power of the Popes. Every time, in his commentaries upon Aristotle, he reached one of those critical points where his philosophy was at variance with the conclusions of Christian theology, John never failed to restate his complete submission to religious orthodoxy, but he usually did it in a rather strange way. In some cases he so obviously enjoys reminding us of all that which he merely believes, and cannot prove, that one wonders what interests him more about those points, that all of them should be believed, or that none of them can be proved. Here is one of those texts:

"I believe and I firmly maintain that the substance of the soul is endowed with natural faculties whose activities are independent from all bodily organs. . . . Such faculties belong in a higher order than that of corporeal matter and far exceed its capacities. . . . And although the soul be united with matter, it nevertheless exercises an (intellectual) activity in which corporeal matter takes no part. All those properties of the soul belong to it truly, simply and absolutely, according to our own faith. And also that an immaterial soul can suffer from a material fire, and be reunited with its own body, after death, by order of the same God Who created it. On the other side, I would not undertake to demonstrate all that, but I think that such things should be believed by simple faith, as well as many others that are to be believed without demonstrative reasons, on the authority of Holy Writ and of miracles. Besides, this is why there is some merit in believing, for the theologians teach us, that there is no merit in believing that which reason can demonstrate." Most of the time, however, John of Jaudun would content himself with cracking some joke, which makes it difficult for his readers to take seriously his most formal professions of faith: "I do believe that that is true; but I cannot prove it. Good luck to those who can!" And again: "I say that God can do that, but how, I don't know; God knows." Another time, after proving at great length that the notion of creation is a philosophical impossibility, John naturally adds that we should nevertheless believe it. Of course, says he, no philosopher ever thought of it, "And no wonder, for it is impossible to reach the notion of creation from the consideration of empirical facts; nor is it possible to justify it by arguments borrowed from sensible experience. And this is why the Ancients, who used to draw their knowledge from rational arguments verified by sensible experience, never succeeded in conceiving such a mode of production." And here is the final stroke: "Let it be added, that creation very seldom happens; there has never been but one, and that was a very long time ago."[9] There was a slight touch of Voltaire in John of Jaudun's irony; and yet, his carefully worded jokes represent only what could then be written; as is usually the case, much more could be said.

In the year 1277, the Bishop of Paris, Etienne Tempier, solemnly condemned 219 propositions either borrowed from Averroistic writings, or expressing current Averroistic opinions. The list of those opinions is a sufficient proof of the fact that pure rationalism was steadily gaining ground around the end of the thirteenth century. Some of those propositions bluntly state, that: "there is no higher life than philosophical life" (*Prop.* 40); or that "there are no wisdoms in the world except that of the philosophers" (*Prop.* 154); and again: "that nothing should be believed, save only that which either is self-evident, or can be deduced from self-evident propositions" (*Prop.* 37). Such statements were just so many challenges to the primacy of Revelation, to the supremacy of Christian Wisdom and to the infallible truth of Revelation. Nor was that all, for some of those propositions went as far as saying that: "Christian Revelation is an obstacle to learning" (*Prop.* 175); and again, that: "one knows nothing more for knowing theology" (*Prop.* 153); and last, not the least, that "Theology rests upon fables" (*Prop.* 152).

Such an Averroism was not that of Averroës

himself, who, at least, entertained a sincere and deep respect for the moralizing power of revealed religions. It had little more in common with the attitude of Siger of Brabant and of Boethius of Dacia, in whose minds simple faith was enough to hold in check the boldest philosophical speculations. As a matter of fact, it was like nothing else in the past, but it anticipated the criticism of the religious dogmas which is a typical feature of the French eighteenth century. That the so-called Revelation is mythical in its origin is everywhere suggested in Fontenelle's *History of the Oracles* (1687); Fontenelle was a very prudent man; he was merely suggesting what he had in mind; but four centuries before him, some Averroists had clearly said it.

The existence of a medieval rationalism should never have been forgotten by those historians who investigate into the origins of the so-called modern rationalism, for indeed the Averroistic tradition forms an uninterrupted chain from the Masters of Arts of Paris and Padua, to the "Libertins" of the seventeenth and of the eighteenth centuries.[10] But it is still more important to remember it, for those who find it easy to sum up in some simple formula six centuries of medieval civilization. What the intellectual life of the Middle Ages might have been if Saint Augustine had never existed, I am not prepared to say; but I feel just as unable to fancy what might have become of it without Averroës and his Latin disciples, not only because they themselves would not have been there, but also because, had they not been there, the work of Saint Thomas Aquinas himself would not have been what it was.

CHAPTER THREE

III

The Harmony of Reason and Revelation

DESPITE their radical opposition, the Theologism and the Rationalism of the thirteenth century had at least one common feature; their onesidedness. Theologism would maintain that every part of Revelation should be understood, while Rationalism would uphold the view that no part of Revelation can be understood. The historical significance of Saint Thomas Aquinas rests with the fact that he was the first medieval thinker to go to the root of the difficulty. It would be quite unfair to his predecessors to forget what they had already done to clear up the problem. Moses Maimonides, the greatest among the Jewish theologians, had clearly defined, in his *Guide for the Perplexed,* the data for a complete solution of the question. Ever since the beginning of the thirteenth century, there had been a growing tendency among the Christian theologians themselves, to draw a dividing line between the order of what we believe and the order of what we know. Alexander of Hales, Saint Bonaventura and still more evidently Saint Albert the Great, had been most insistent on the fundamental importance of that distinction. But the real reformer is not the man who sees that a reform is needed; nor is he the man who, in season and out of season, preaches the necessity of that reform; the true reformer is the man who achieves it.

Saint Thomas Aquinas was wonderfully equipped to solve a problem of that kind, because it was a problem of order. Now anyone who is at all familiar with his work knows full well that he simply could not help putting everything in its proper place. Each thing in its own place, a place for each thing. Now, in everyday life, the problem of putting a thing in its proper place is a comparatively simple one. It seldom amounts to more than putting it always in the same place and remembering where it is. Not so in philosophy, where there is but one conceivable proper place for any given thing. Unless you find it, that thing is lost, not in the usual sense that it is not to be found where you expected it to be, but in the much more radical sense that it is no longer to be found anywhere. Out of its proper place, the thing simply cannot exist at all. For indeed, the place of each thing is determined there by its own essence, and unless you know first what the thing is you shall never be able to define its relations to what it is not.

When stated as an abstract principle, the general idea of such a method is easy enough to understand; but nobody can apply it to concrete cases unless he be possessed of two intellectual qualities, whose combination in the same mind is rather rare: a perfect intellectual modesty and an almost reckless intellectual audacity. Now Saint Thomas Aquinas had both in an uncommonly high degree. He had intellectual modesty, because he always began by accepting things just as they were. Thomas Aquinas never expected that things would conform themselves to his own definitions of them; quite the reverse, what he would call the true knowledge of a thing was the adequate intellectual expression of the thing such as it is in itself. But he had also intellectual audacity, for, after accepting a thing such as it was, he would insist on dealing with it according to its own nature, and he would do it fearlessly, without compromise. In the present case, the trouble was that some theologians wanted to theologize in philosophy, whereas some philosophers wanted to philosophize in theology. Consequently, the only way to bring that strife to a close was for Saint Thomas Aquinas to handle philosophical problems as a philosopher and theological problems as a theologian.

In order to clear up the difficulty, let us begin by defining the proper nature of religious faith. To have faith is to assent to something because it is revealed by God. And now, what is it to have science? It is to assent to something which we perceive as true in the natural light of reason. The essential difference between these two distinct orders of assent should be carefully kept in mind by anybody dealing with the relations of Reason and Revelation. I know by reason that something is true because *I see* that it is true; but I believe that something is true because *God has said it*. In those two cases the cause of my assent is specifically different, consequently science and faith should be held as two specifically different kinds of assent.

If they are two distinct species of knowledge, we should never ask one of them to fulfil what is the proper function of the other. We should never do it for the simple reason that, since they are specifically distinct, one of them cannot possibly be the other one. For instance, I cannot possibly ask you to believe that I am here; you cannot believe it, because you see it. On the other hand, I cannot cause you to see that I am now interpreting for you the fifth article of the second section of the second Part of the *Summa Theologica* of Saint Thomas Aquinas. I can only ask you to believe it. Later on, if you check up my reference, you will see whether I was right or wrong in quoting it; and then you will know whether I was right or wrong, but it will become impossible for you to believe it. Now the same distinction should apply to the problem of reason and Revelation. According to its very definition, faith implies assent of the intellect to that which the intellect does not see to be true, either as one of the first principles, or as one of their necessary conclusions. Consequently, an act of faith cannot be caused by a rational evidence, but entails an intervention of the will. On the contrary, in scientific knowledge, my assent is sufficiently and completely determined by its very object. Whence there follows that, in Thomas Aquinas' own words, since "it is impossible that one and the same thing should be believed and seen by the same person, . . . it is equally impossible for one and the same thing to be an object of science and of belief for the same person." In short, one and the same thing cannot be at one and the same time both an object of science and an object of faith.

When we read those lines, what they say seems to be pretty obvious; and, in a way, it was; yet those simple statements are a landmark in the history of western thought. By taking such a stand, Thomas Aquinas was challenging the distinction more or less confusedly implied in so many theologies, between the simple faith of common people, and the enlightened faith of the *meliores*, who add to faith its understanding.[1] It is typical of Saint Thomas Aquinas that he could not tolerate even the shadow of such a confusion: "that which is proposed to be believed equally by all is unknown by all as an object of science: such are the things which are of faith simply." Consequently, if we are dealing with those things which are essentially of faith, it becomes absurd to draw any distinction between the mass of the simple believers and the aristocracy of those who add to the same faith its understanding. As believers, all Christians are in the same predicament, for all of them agree as to what they believe, and none of them has any scientific knowledge of it.

What then should we answer, when great theologians, who sometimes are also great saints, enjoin us to accept their reasons as necessary demonstrations of what we hold as true by faith? Simply that it cannot be done. The authority of so high a saint and of so great a theologian as Saint Anselm himself has absolutely nothing to do with the question. In fact, "the reasons employed by holy men to prove things that are of faith are not demonstrations." And why? Because they cannot be. If that which they pretend to demonstrate were really demonstrated, it would become scientifically known and therefore could no longer be believed.[2]

Saint Thomas did not content himself with a mere abstract statement of his general answer to the question, he applied it to the solution of many particular problems. And no wonder, for in all those cases the very nature of Revelation, of faith and of theology itself was at stake. In its own way, theology itself is a science, whose conclusions necessarily follow from their principles; but those principles are articles of faith, and faith itself is an assent to the word of God accepted as word of God. Were we to say, on the contrary, that there are necessary demonstrations of the revealed truth, we could no longer believe in it, there would be no articles of faith, no principles of theological reasoning, no theology conceived as a distinct order of knowledge. In other words, revealed theology, or the theology of Revelation, would disappear as religious knowledge; what would be left in its place would be natural theology, that is to say, metaphysics.

Such was the fundamental reason why Saint Thomas Aquinas never failed to stress the transcendent nature and incomparable dignity of the word of God every time he could find some appropriate occasion to do it. If it is of the essence of an article of faith to rest upon divine authority alone, its would-be demonstrations cannot possibly be necessary demonstrations. Now our faith in Revelation should not be a merely natural assent to some rational probability. When something is rationally probable, its contrary also is rationally probable. It is but an opinion. Religious faith is not an opinion. It is the unshakable certitude that God has spoken, and that what God has said is true, even though we do not understand it. Hence Thomas Aquinas' repeated warnings not to overrate the value of such probabilities, lest, as he himself says, "the Catholic faith seem to be founded on empty reasonings, and not, as it is, on the most solid teaching of God."[3] And again: "And it is useful to consider this, lest anyone, presuming to demonstrate what is of faith, should bring forward reasons that are not cogent, so as to give occasion to unbelievers to laugh, and to think that such are the grounds on which we believe things that are of faith."[4]

By thus excluding from theology all necessary demonstrations of purely rational nature, Thomas Aquinas was cutting loose from the theologism of the early Middle Ages. From now on, and up to our own days, there have always been men to maintain that Revelation is a self-sufficient and self-contained order of truth, whose ultimate foundation is divine authority alone and not the natural light of reason. This, however, should immediately be added, that the specific distinction introduced by Thomas Aquinas between faith and rational knowledge was not understood by him as a separation, still less as an Averroistic opposition. To those professors of philosophy who deemed it expedient to state their conclusions as necessary, but not as true, Thomas Aquinas objected that their position was an impossible one. In describing their authentic attitude, we had to stress the fact that no Averroist could be quoted as having said that he believed by faith as true the very reverse of what he knew by necessary reasons to be true. We even added that, psychologically speaking, theirs was by no means an inconceivable attitude. But Thomas Aquinas was right in pointing to the fact that their philosophical position involved a latent absurdity.

Just as Averroës himself, Thomas Aquinas felt convinced that nothing should enter the texture of metaphysical knowledge save only rational and necessary demonstrations. For the same reason, he even agreed with Averroës that the so-called necessary reasons of so many theologians were mere dialectical probabilities. As he once said of such arguments, they never convince anyone unless he already believes what they are supposed to prove. Moreover, Thomas Aquinas had in common with Averroës an immense admiration for Aristotle, whose fundamental principles he certainly identified with those of natural reason itself. As to Averroës, he was to Thomas Aquinas what he was to everybody else in the Middle Ages: the Commentator *par excellence*. Yet Saint Thomas never considered Averroës as a faultless interpreter of Aristotle, nor Aristotle himself as an infallible philosopher. The attitude of the Latin Averroists was an altogether different one. Whereas Thomas Aquinas would follow Aristotle when he was right, but no further, and because he was right, but on no other ground, the Averroists would consider Averroës, Aristotle and human reason, as three different words for one and the same thing. That surprising attitude does not account only for the philosophical sterility of their school as a whole, but also for the passive resignation of some of them between the antinomies of Christian faith and of natural reason. Convinced, as they were, that not a word could be altered in the works of Averroës without wrecking philosophy itself, they could do but one of two things: either drop their religious beliefs, in which case there was nothing left to harmonize, or else accept contradiction as a normal condition of the human mind.

Saint Thomas Aquinas did his very best to convince them that their ill-guided devotion to the letter of what they took to be philosophy was indeed destructive of philosophy. To say that the conclusions of Averroës were rationally necessary, but not necessarily true, was to empty the word "truth" of all meaning. If that which appears as necessary in the light of natural reason cannot be posited as true, what else will be posited as true in philosophy? That which is not contradicted by Revelation? But if rational evidence falls short of the truth in a single case it becomes meaningless in all the others. Hence Saint Thomas' own interpretation and refutation of their position. If what is rationally necessary is thereby necessarily true, those Averroists were actually teaching a doctrine of the twofold truth; they were maintaining as simultaneously true two sets of contradictory propositions.

By bringing together the results of the two distinct criticisms directed by Thomas Aquinas against the theologism of Saint Anselm and the Averroism of Siger de Brabant, we begin to discern the general features of a third position on the problem, as well as of a third spiritual family, that of the Thomists. All its members will grant that there is a true Revelation: the Christian Revelation. They grant it, but they do not take it for granted. No man would ever admit that God has spoken, unless he had solid proofs of the fact. Such proofs are to be found in history, where the miracles of God, and quite especially the greatest of all: the life and growth of His Church, prove His presence, the truth of His doctrine and the permanence of His inspiration. If truly God has spoken, His Revelation must needs be true, and it is necessary for us to believe it. For this is the proper aim and scope of Revelation to provide all men, philosophers or not, with such a knowledge of God, of man and of his destiny, as is required for their eternal salvation. Now, that knowledge itself is made up of several different elements, among which two main classes should be carefully distinguished. The first one comprises a certain number of revealed truths which, though they be revealed, are nevertheless attainable by reason alone. Such are, for instance, the existence of God and His essential attributes, or the existence of the human soul and its immortality. Why did God reveal to men even some truths which natural reason could attain? Because very few men are metaphysicians, whereas all men need to be saved. By revealing them to mankind, God has enabled each of us to know the whole saving truth immediately, with absolute certitude and in its perfect purity.[5] Yet, any part of Revelation which is attainable by natural reason should be considered rather as a necessary presupposition to matters of faith than as an article of faith properly said.[6] Only those men who cannot see its truth in the light of reason are held in conscience to accept it by simple faith. The second group of revealed truths contains all the articles of faith properly said, that is to say, all that part of the Revelation which surpasses the whole range of human reason. Such are, for instance, the Trinity, the Incarnation and the Redemption. No philosophical speculation can give any necessary reason in favor of any truth of that kind; no philosophical conclusions can be deduced from any articles of faith, for they are believed principles of equally believed theological consequences, not intelligible principles of demonstrated rational conclusions. Yet, if reason cannot prove them to be true, it cannot either prove them to be false. Quite the reverse. To any sincere believer who is at the same time a true philosopher, the slightest opposition between his faith and his reason is a sure sign that something is the matter with his philosophy. For indeed faith is not a principle of philosophical knowledge, but it is a safe guide to rational truth and an infallible warning against philosophical error. A man who does not like to believe what he can know, and who never pretends to know what can be but believed, and yet a man whose faith and knowledge grow into an organic unity because they both spring from the same divine source, such is, if not the portrait, at least a sketch of the typical member of the Thomist family. Cajetan and John of Saint Thomas were men of that type and still today one of its finest specimens can be found amongst us, in the person of M. Jacques Maritain.

Had it been given to Thomas Aquinas to convince, if not his own contemporaries, at least his immediate successors, the intellectual and moral crisis would have soon come to a close, and the whole history of western thought would have been different from what it was. Unfortunately, the net result of Averroës' influence was to breed in the minds of the theologians a growing mistrust for philosophy. If that was natural reason, Revelation would be better off without its help than with it. Hence, in even the greatest among the late medieval philosophers and theologians, an increasing tendency to ascribe to faith alone, not only what Thomas Aquinas would call the articles of faith properly said, but even what we saw him define as rational preambles to matters of faith. It thus came to pass that the list of the revealed truths that can be either believed, or proven, was steadily growing shorter and shorter to the point of shrivelling into nothingness. A typical instance of that historical phenomenon can be found, within the Thomist school itself, in the person of no less a man than Cardinal Cajetan, one of the greatest commentators of Saint Thomas Aquinas. Cajetan entertained grave doubts as to the power of natural reason to demonstrate the immortality of the soul, and consequently the existence of future rewards and punishments. But Cajetan was writing in the sixteenth century and, by that time, the other theological schools had already followed the same road up to its very end.

As early as the last years of the thirteenth century, Duns Scotus had considerably increased the list of those revealed truths which a Christian should believe, but cannot prove. At the end of his treatise *On the First Principle*, Duns Scotus expressly states that the all-powerfulness of God, His immensity, His omnipresence, His providence,

His justice and His *miséricord* towards all creatures, but especially towards man, are as many beliefs not susceptible of rational demonstration. Should the famous *Theoremata* be ascribed to him, the list of those undemonstrable propositions would become a considerably longer one. But the point is immaterial to the problem at stake. Whoever wrote the *Theoremata*, often ascribed to Duns Scotus, the fact remains that their author listed among the undemonstrable propositions, besides the preceding ones, the unicity of God, the creation of the world out of nothingness, and its present conservation by the same God who once created it. True enough, all such articles of faith can be proved in theology by rational and necessary demonstrations; that is, they can be proved provided they be believed first; but philosophical reason alone utterly fails to prove them.

The next step along the same line was taken by the English Franciscan, William of Ockham, in the first third of the fourteenth century. A bitter opponent of Duns Scotus, Ockham always maintained that absolutely nothing could be proved about God in the light of natural reason, not even

His existence. To him, as to Averröes, what reason can say concerning theological matters never goes beyond the order of mere dialectical probability. It is indeed probable that there is a God, who created the heaven and the earth; it is also probable that man has been endowed by God with a soul, and that, being an uncorporeal substance, that soul is immortal. Ockham would look at such propositions not only as probable ones, but as distinctly more probable than their contraries. Yet, none of them could be demonstrated in philosophy, and consequently, in spite of all that Anselm and Duns Scotus could say to the contrary, they could not be demonstrated even in theology. In short, they could not be demonstrated at all.

The influence of Ockham is everywhere present in the fourteenth century; it progressively invaded Oxford, Paris, and practically all the European universities. Some would profess it, others would refute it, but nobody was allowed to ignore it. The late Middle Ages were then called upon to witness the total wreck of both scholastic philosophy and scholastic theology as the necessary upshot of the final divorce of reason and Revelation. Granted that not a single one of the revealed truths could possibly be justified by natural reason, why should pious souls have paid the slightest attention to philosophy? It could do no good, but it could do infinite harm to most of those who studied it. I wonder how many among the readers of the *Imitation of Christ* are conscious of reading a late medieval protest against the vanity of all philosophy? Very few, I suppose, and I would not blame the other ones, for the true greatness of the book does not lie there. Yet, whoever he was, the author of that famous treatise was certainly no great admirer of philosophers, nor even of theologians. "If you knew the whole Bible by heart," he says in the very first chapter of his book, "and the sayings of all the philosophers, what would that profit you without the love of God and grace? Vanity of vanities, all is vanity, save to love God and to serve Him only." (*Imit.* I: 1, 10–11.) Again, "The time shall come when the Teacher of teachers, Christ, the Lord of Angels, shall appear to hear the lessons of all, that is, to examine the consciences of each one; and then He shall search Jerusalem with candles, and the hidden things of darkness shall be manifest, and the arguing of men's tongues shall be silent. I am he who exalteth in a moment the humble mind, to comprehend more reasonings of the eternal truth than if one had studied ten years in the schools." (*Imit.* III:43, 10–11.)[7]

It is a blessing for all of us that the problem of who wrote the *Imitation* does not fall within the scope of the present inquiry. Several different writers have been made responsible for that book, and I happen to be personally acquainted with four historians who have discovered its true author; unfortunately, no two of them have discovered the same. But I hasten to add that, in so far as I can see, many other names have been quoted or could be quoted without absurdity. Here again we find ourselves confronted with a more or less definite group of kindred minds, whose answers to the problem of faith and reason were substantially the same. As early as the fifteenth century their common attitude had already been given a name: the *Moderna devotio*, that is, the modern, or new devotion. All the best historians of that movement agree at least on this, that it expressed a feeling of lassitude, after the failure of so many philosophers and theologians to achieve anything like a commonly received truth. Duns Scotus had disagreed with Thomas Aquinas and Ockham had disagreed with Duns Scotus. Whom should one believe? True enough, the masters of mystical life had found a way out of that maze in what they called the union of the soul with God. But had they really found it? Meister Eckhart's doctrine had been condemned by Pope John XXII in 1329; John Ruysbroeck was being accused of Averroism by John Gerson, who himself was not without a smacking of Occamism. Many fourteenth-century Christians were simply fed up with the whole business. They had no use for speculative theology, they would not loose themselves into the obscure and unsafe mysteries of mystical union; what they wanted was straight practical Christian life, and nothing else. Gehrard Groote (Gerritt Groot) was prompted by such a motive when, in 1381, he established in Deventer the fraternity of the *Brethren of the Common Life*. Gehrard Groote is one of the possible authors of the *Imitation of Christ*. Near Deventer, and in close relations with the *Brethren of the Common Life*, was the monastery of the Canons

Regular of Windesheim; one of its Priors, John Vos de Huesden, has left us a "conférence" whose doctrine closely resembles that of the *Imitation.* One of the most popular candidates to the title, Thomas à Kempis, had been educated at Deventer.[8] But it should not be forgotten that though the odds seem now to be against him, John Gerson has long been a favorite. Now, when historians want to describe his fundamental attitude, what do they call it? A "reaction from excessive speculation."[9] From whatever angle we may choose to consider the then existing situation, nothing can be seen there, save only lassitude and discouragement.

When the best minds began to despair of harmonizing the teachings of Christian Revelation with those of philosophy, the end of the Middle Ages was at hand. In 1475, a twelve-year-old boy entered the school of the *Brethren of the Common Life.* His name was Desiderius Erasmus. One of the greatest among the great figures of the Renaissance, Erasmus was nevertheless a perfect expression of the fourteenth-century reaction against both scholastic philosophy and scholastic theology. Or rather, what is usually considered as a typical feature of the early Renaissance is but the normal development of a tendency, probably as old as Christianity itself, but whose immediate origins are to be found way back in the first years of the fourteenth century. 'Away with philosophy,' and 'Back to the Gospel,' such was, in a nutshell, the doctrine of Erasmus in his *Paraclesis* (1516), and in his *Ratio seu methodus perveniendi ad veram philosophiam* (1518). A long time before him, Petrarch had already said pretty much the same thing. What we call the "Christian humanism" of the Renaissance owes its final triumph to the marvellous talent of Erasmus; but the medieval founders of the *New Devotion* had laid down the very premises whence their pupil Erasmus was to draw his conclusions.

Nor is that all. Among the typical expressions of the medieval reaction from excessive speculation, special mention should be made of another anonymous treatise, written by some German theologian in the course of the fourteenth century: the so-called *Theologia deutsch*, that is, a *German Theology*.[10] Martin Luther published it for the first time in 1516, then again in 1518, this time with an enthusiastic Preface, where he went as far as saying: "I declare that I have not found any book, except the Bible and Saint Augustine, which has taught me more of the meaning of God, Christ, man, and everything."[11] Even taking into account the lack of aptness at understatement so often betrayed by Luther's writings, the fact remains that his discovery of the *Theologia deutsch* marks an important date in his religious evolution. What delighted him in that treatise was its complete indifference to speculative theology. Now Luther himself was well trained in scholastic theology[12] but he hated it as being destructive of simple faith and therefore of Christianity itself. It is significant that in 1517, that is, just a year after the publishing of the *German Theology*, Luther entrusted one of his students with the task of publicly disputing against scholastic theology. In this important document, the bitterness of innumerable priests, monks, preachers and University professors that, for two centuries at least, had been accumulating against scholastic philosophy, found at last its complete expression. "The whole of Aristotle," Luther says, "is to theology as darkness is to light. Against

Scholasticism." And to those who go on repeating, "Nobody becomes a theologian without Aristotle," Luther answers: "Quite the reverse: only without Aristotle can we become theologians."[13]

If the *New Devotion* can be truly considered as having, if not caused, at least occasioned, the Lutheran spirituality on the one side and the Christian humanism of Erasmus on the other side, its significance for the history of the Renaissance, and therefore of modern times themselves, should no longer be neglected by any thoughtful historian. Now, the rise of that *New Devotion* itself was largely ascribable to the disruption of the Thomistic synthesis under the lasting pressure of Averroës and of the Latin Averroists. Thus understood, the history of western thought from the thirteenth up to the sixteenth centuries begins to assume some sort of intelligibility. What was new at the times of the Renaissance still appears as having then been new, but we see it rooted in a medieval past by which alone it can be explained. After the Reformers and the Humanists, the men of the sixteenth century found themselves confronted with a theology without philosophy: the *positive* or *modern* philosophy of Fr. de Vitoria and of M. Cano; and a philosophy without theology: the purely rational speculation of R. Descartes and of Francis Bacon. In the light of our previous analyses, how could we fail to perceive that the so-called modern conditions of both theology and philosophy were the practically unavoidable upshot of at least two centuries of medieval speculation? For indeed, between the harmony of faith and reason as achieved by Thomas Aquinas and their radical divorce, there was no room left for an intermediate position.

If it be true that in spite of its slow and fluctuating evolution the history of ideas is determined from within by the internal necessity of ideas themselves, the conclusions of our inquiry should exhibit a more than historical value. Wherever and whenever the problem of the relations of faith and reason may happen to be asked, the abstract conditions of its solution are bound to remain the same. Now it should not be forgotten that, even in our own days, the question is very far from being out of date. If, thirty years ago, anybody had asked himself the question: Who are the two leading philosophers of our own times? his answer would have been: W. James and H. Bergson. In point of fact, we learn from Professor R. B. Perry's admirable biography of W. James, that "the first conjunction of those two luminaries took place on May 28, 1905." We know from Bergson himself how the two great thinkers greeted one another: "I believe that we did indeed say '*Bonjour*,' but that was all; there were several instants of silence, and straightway he asked me how I envisaged the problem of religion."[14]

The *Varieties of Religious Experience* and the *Twofold Sources of Ethics and Religion* are there, as irrecusable witnesses to their seriousness of purpose. It would be neither intelligent nor fair to deal in five minutes with such philosophical masterpieces; but I cannot help feeling that both books would be still greater than they actually are if their conclusions had taken into account seven centuries of historical experience. It is psychologically interesting to know that it does one good to *believe* there is a God; but that is not at all what the believer believes; what he actually believes is, that there *is* a God. The problem of religion requires that there is some being to which we must be bound;

and the problem of Revelation requires that there is some divinely made statement to which we must bow. I am not at all denying the intrinsic validity of the other attitudes, but I beg to stress the fact that, useful and instructive as they may prove to be, they finally leave out the religious problem itself. Indeed, they cannot even ask it. After reading W. James, I still want to know if my religious experience is an experience of God, or an experience of myself. For in both cases there can be a psychological religious experience, but in the first case only can there be a religion. Similarly, I can follow Bergson in his description of mystical intuition as a source of religious life, but even after reading him, I am still wondering what the nature of that intuition actually is. Is it a self-sufficient intuition of an object which may also be the object of religious faith, or is it an experience in faith and through faith of the God in whom we believe?

Here again, the matter is an important one, and the solution is bound to qualify all that can be said on that question. This is so true, that despite their cleverness in avoiding, as unphilosophical, the problem of an historical Revelation of God to men, even contemporary philosophers are driven back to it by the very nature of the question. How indeed could they help it? The very meaning of the problem itself is at stake. As Bergson himself says: "At the origin of Christianity, there is Christ."[15] Likewise, after painstakingly describing in his book what he calls the "inner witness of the Holy Spirit," Rudolf Otto warns us, in his last page, that above that witness, there is the Prophet, and that, above the Prophet, there is such a one as is more than Prophet. The four last words of the book at last tell us who he is: "He is the Son."[16]

There, I think, the real question begins. Knowing, as we do, that He who is more than Prophet has spoken, what are we to do with His message? If what His message says does at times escape the grasp of natural reason, what is natural reason going to say about it? Once we have reached that point, God can no longer be conceived by us as a mere "wholly other" to which our *a priori* category of the "Numinous" bears witness; the Son also is a witness, and He has said who the Father is. That, at last, is a Revelation worthy of the name: not our own revelation of God to ourselves, but the

Revelation of God Himself to us. Such are the only conceivable terms of the real problem, and since they are identically the same as those of the medieval problem, it would be a wise thing to do, for any one interested in solving it, to become acquainted with the writings of medieval theologians. For there is at least one thing that we still can learn from them concerning that question, and this is the correct way to ask it. So long as we ask no more than to harmonize our own religious feelings with our private impression of philosophical knowledge, we are still very far from encountering the real difficulty. If, on the contrary, we learn from medieval theologians what is faith in an objective truth and what is an objective philosophical knowledge, we shall find ourselves possessed of both a Revelation and a Reason. There then will be something to harmonize, and anyone attempting to do it will end at last in meeting the real problem. But he can scarcely avoid meeting Saint Thomas Aquinas.

NOTES

Notes

[Pp. 8-13]

CHAPTER I

(1) As a general introduction to the question, see TH. HEITZ, *Essai historique sur les rapports entre la philosophie et la foi, de Bérenger de Tours à saint Thomas d'Aquin,* Gabalda, Paris, 1909. See also M. GRABMANN, *Die Geschichte der scholastischen Methode,* Herder, Freiburg i. Br., 2 vols., 1909. E. GILSON, *The Spirit of Mediæval Philosophy,* transl. by A. H. C. Downes, Scribner, New York, 1936. The best reference book for general information concerning medieval philosophers, their works, lives and doctrines, is FRIED. UEBERWEGS, *Grundriss der Geschichte der Philosophie,* Pt. II: *Die patristische und scholastische Philosophie,* edit. by B. Geyer, Mittler, Berlin, 1928. The best summary of the history of medieval theology is that of M. GRABMANN, *Die Geschichte der Katholischen Theologie seit dem Ausgang der Väterzeit,* Herder, Freiburg i. Br., 1933; pp. 1–133.

(2) TERTULLIAN, *On Prescription against Heretics,* Ch. VII; in *The Ante-Nicene Fathers,* Buffalo, 1887; Vol. III, p. 246. Cf. J. LÖRTZ, *Tertullian ab Apologet,* Aschendorff, Münster i. Westf., 1927. For an easily available text, see TERTULLIAN, *On the Testimony of the Soul* and *On the 'Prescription' of Heretics,* transl. by T. H. Bindley, S.P.C.K., London, 1914.

(3) TATIAN, *Address to the Greeks,* in *The Ante-Nicene Fathers,* Buffalo, 1885; Vol. II, Ch. II, p. 65, and Ch. XXXII, p. 78. Cf. A. PUECH, *Recherches sur le Discours aux Grecs de Tatien,* F. Alcan, Paris, 1903.

(4) SAINT BERNARD, *op. cit.,* in *St. Bernard's Sermons for the seasons and principal festivals of the year,* transl. by a Priest of Mount Melleray, Dublin, Browne and

Nolan, 1923; Vol. II, pp. 310 & 311. Cf. E. Gilson, *La théologie mystique de saint Bernard,* J. Vrin, Paris, 1934.

(5) On Peter Damiani, see J. A. Endres, *Petrus Damiani und die weltliche Wissenschaft,* Aschendorff, Münster i. Westf., 1910. Cf. E. Gilson, *Études de philosophie médiévale,* Strasbourg, 1921; pp. 31–38.

(6) I am quoting from the rhythmical rendering, in Anne Macdonell, *Sons of Francis,* London, J. M. Dent, and N. Y., G. P. Putnam's Sons, 1902; p. 369. More texts to the same effect will be found in the same chapter, pp. 354–386.

(7) The passage is translated in: J. Sighart, *Albert the Great, O.P., his Life and Scholastic Labours,* London, R. Washbourne, 1876; Ch. VII, pp. 85–86. Even as late as the XVIIth century, Francis Bacon had to take into account the existence and activity of those more zealous than enlightened theologians, as can be seen from his book *On the Advancement of Learning,* I, 2. The "fundamentalists" are an undying race; like the Jebusites, they cannot be exterminated.

Cf. Gilb. Murray, *Five Stages of Greek Religion,* Columbia Univ. Press, 1925.

(8) Saint Augustine, *On the Gospel of Saint John,* XXIX, 6; in *Homilies on the Gospel of St. John,* transl. by H. Browne, J. H. Parker (A Library of Fathers), Oxford, 1848; Vol. I, p. 440.

(9) Saint Augustine, *On free will,* II, 2, 6; as translated in E. Przywara, *An Augustine Synthesis,* N. Y., Sheed and Ward, 1936; pp. 58–59. Other texts of Augustine on the same subject will be found in the same book, pp. 41–58: *From understanding to faith;* and pp. 58–67: *From faith to understanding.* Cf. J. Maritain, *St. Augustine and St. Thomas Aquinas,* transl. by Fr. Leonard, in *A Monument to Saint Augustine,* Sheed and Ward, London, 1930, pp. 199–223.

(10) Thomas Aquinas, *Summa Theologica,* Pt. I, qu. 84, art. 5, Answer; transl. by the Fathers of the English

Dominican Province, p. 171: "Consequently whenever Augustine, who was imbued with the doctrines of the Platonists . . ." etc.

(11) E. Gilson, *Introduction à l'étude de saint Augustin,* J. Vrin, Paris, 1929, pp. 86–137. Other approaches to the same problem will be found in J. Hessen, *Augustins Metaphysik der Erkenntnis,* F. Dümmler, Berlin, 1931; and F. Cayré, *La contemplation augustinienne,* A. Blot, Paris, 1927.

(12) Saint Anselm, *Monologium,* Preface; transl. by S. N. Deane, The Open Court Co., Chicago, 1935, p. 36; and *Proslogium,* Preface, pp. 6–7.

(13) Gaunilo, *Liber pro insipiente, ibid.* Cf. the text and its French translation in A. Koyré, *St. Anselme de Canterbéry, Fides quaerens intellectum,* J. Vrin, Paris, 1930.

(14) Saint Anselm, *Cur Deus homo,* Preface; we are partly following S. N. Deane's translation, pp. 177-178.

(15) Roger Bacon, *Opus majus,* Pt. IV, Dist. 1, Ch. 1; in R. B. Burke's translation, Philadelphia, Univ. of Pennsylvania Press, 1928; Vol. I, pp. 123–124.

(16) Roger Bacon, *Opus majus,* Pt. IV, Dist. 4: *The application of mathematics to sacred subjects;* Vol. I, pp. 238–242.

(17) Roger Bacon, *Opus majus,* Pt. VI, Ch. 2; Vol. II, pp. 586–587. On that important aspect of Bacon's doctrine, see the remarkable book of R. Carton, *L'expérience mystique de l'illumination intérieure chez Roger Bacon,* J. Vrin, Paris, 1924.

(18) Cf. the shorter redaction of Lull's *Ars magna,* published by Carm. Ottaviano, *L'Ars compendiosa de R. Lulle,* J. Vrin, Paris, 1930.

(19) E. A. Peers, *Ramon Lull, a Biography,* S.P.C.K., London, 1929; pp. 312–313. A very valuable introduction to the study of Lull.

CHAPTER II

(1) The arabic text of the *Theology of Aristotle* has been published and translated into German, by Fr. Dieterici, *Die sogenannte Theologie des Aristoteles aus arabischen Handschriften zum erstenmal herausgegeben;* J. C. Hinrich, Leipzig, 1882.

The gothic editions of Avicenna are very difficult to find; but there is an easily available abridgment of his *Metaphysics,* written by Avicenna himself, and translated into Latin by Nem. Carame, *Avicennae Metaphysices Compendium,* Pontif. Inst. Orient. Stud., Rome; no date. Another, still more complete restatement of Avicenna's philosophy can be found in the Latin medieval translation of *Algazel's Metaphysics, a Mediæval Translation,* edit. by J. T. Muckle, Sheed and Ward, New York, 1933. Cf. M. Horten, *Die Metaphysik Avicennas, enthaltend die Metaphysik, Theologie, Kosmologie und Ethic, übersetzt und erlautert;* R. Haupt, Halle a.S. und New York, 1907. D. J. Saliba, *Étude sur la métaphysique d'Avicenne,* Presses Universitaires, Paris, 1926.

Asin Palacios, *Algazel: Dogmatica, moral, ascetica* (Coleccion de estudios arab., Vol. VI), Comas, Zaragoza, 1901. Carra de Vaux, *Gazali,* F. Alcan, Paris, 1902.

Cf. Dante's famous verse:

> Euclide geometra, e Tolomeo,
> Ippocrate, Avicenna e Galieno:
> Averrois, che'l gran commento feo.
> (*Inf.* IV, 142–144.)

Averroës is quoted here from L. Gauthier, *Accord de la religion et de la philosophie,* traduit et annoté, Imprimérie orientale Fontana, Alger, 1905, pp. 18–20. The arabic text has been published and translated into German by M. J. Müller, *Philosophie und Theologie von Averroës,* München, 1859. An English translation of the same work has been published in India by M. Jamil-Ur-Rehman, *The Philosophy of Averroës,* Baroda, 1921. For a detailed study of the problem, see E. RENAN, *Averroës et l'Averroisme, Essai historique,* Calmann-Lévy, Paris, 1852, and several later editions. In the third edition (1866), see esp. pp. 162–172; and L. GAUTHIER, *La théorie d'Ibn Rochd (Averroës) sur les rapports de la religion et de la philosophie,* E. Leroux, Paris, 1903; esp. pp. 177–182.

(2) AVERROËS, *Accord de la religion . . .,* pp. 21–26.

(3) AVERROËS, *Accord de la religion . . .,* p. 26.

(4) E. RENAN, *Averroës et l'Averroisme,* pp. 162–172, and the criticism (itself criticizable, but suggestive) of Renan's position, by L. GAUTHIER, *La théorie d'Ibn Rochd . . .,* pp. 1–18 and pp. 177–182.

(5) AVERROËS, *Accord de la religion . . .,* pp. 50–51.

(6) AVERROËS, *Accord de la religion . . .,* pp. 51–52. In the above-mentioned English translation, pp. 243–257.

The treatise of Averroës on the *Harmony of religion and philosophy* remained unknown to the Christian Theologians of the Middle Ages; but the last chapter of Averroës' *Destruction* contains a summary of his ideas on the question, and it was translated into Latin in the first third of the XIVth century. Cf. AVERROËS, *Destructio destructionum,* Disput. V, printed in the edition of Venice, apud Juntas, 1550, Vol. IX, f° 63.

(7) On the so-called doctrine of the twofold truth in Latin Averroism, see E. GILSON, *La doctrine de la double vérité,* in *Études de philosophie médiévale,* Strasbourg, 1921, pp. 50–69. In the very same year, and quite independently from the preceding article, an Italian scholar was reaching identically the same conclusion; cf. BRUNO NARDI, *Intorno alle dottrine filosofiche di Pietro d'Abano,* in Nuova Rivista Storica, Albrighi Segati, Milano, Vol. V, 2–3 (1921), pp. 34–35, and pp. 48–49.

(8) Dante has placed Siger of Brabant in his *Paradiso* (*Div. Comedy,* Parad., X, 133–138). The presence of a so well-known Averroist in Dante's heaven has given rise to endless controversies. The best explanation of that fact

seems to be that of Br. Nardi, viz. that Dante himself being something of an Averroist, he could have no objections to Siger of Brabant (Br. Nardi, *Saggi de Filosofia Dantesca,* Socanon Edit., Dante Alighieri, Milano, 1930). There would be serious difficulty in admitting that conclusion, if the texts recently published by Fr. Van Steenberghen under the name of Siger could really be ascribed to him; but the internal evidence is against it and the external evidence is very weak, not to say non-existent. Cf. Br. Nardi's article in *Giornale critico della filosofia italiana,* 1936, pp. 26–35. An answer to Br. Nardi's criticism is announced by Fr. Van Steenberghen, in *Revue Néoscolastique de Philosophie,* Vol. 40 (1937), pp 142–144.

See G. de Lagarde, *La naissance de l'esprit laique au déclin du moyen age,* Vol. II: *Marsile de Padoue ou le premier théoricien de l'ésprit laique,* Editions Béatrice, Saint-Paul-Trois-Chateaux, 1934.

(9) Those texts of John of Jaudun, together with several other ones, have been collected in E. Gilson, *Études de philosophie médiévale,* Strasbourg, 1921; pp. 70–75.

(10) On the continuity of the Averroistic tradition, see: E. Renan, *Averroës et l'Averroisme;* Paris, 1852. R. Charbonnel, *La pensée italienne au XVIe siecle et le courant libertin;* Paris, Picard, 1904. H. Busson, *Les sources et le développement du rationalisme dans la littérature française de la Renaissance* (1533–1601). Paris, Letouzey et Ané, 1922.

CHAPTER III

(1) The Gnostic distinction between Faith, considered as an inferior type of religious knowledge, and the Gnosis, considered as an intellectual experience of religious truth, has never been accepted by any Father of the Church or medieval theologian; to them, there was but one Catholic faith, the same for all Christians, and one to

which the assent of the most learned theologians was just as strictly bound as that of the most illiterate people. Yet, Clement of Alexandria, for instance, certainly admitted of a hierarchy, if not of beliefs, at least of believers. His "Christian Gnostic" believes the same things as all the other Christians, but his own faith is crowned by a religious "knowledge" which is refused to common believers (see the texts collected in G. Bardy, *Clément d'Alexandrie,* J. Gabalda, Paris, 1926; pp. 246–312). A slight touch of that aristocratic religious feeling can still be detected in an early text of Saint Augustine: "nam et a *melioribus* etiam dum has terras incolunt, et certe a bonis et piis omnibus post hanc vitam . . ." (*De libero arbitrio,* II, 2, 6). All good and pious men (*omnes*) will see God in future life, but the *meliores* can already *know* something about Him.

(2) Thomas Aquinas, *Summa Theologica,* Pt. II^{a}–II^{ae}, qu. I, art. 5; transl. by the Fathers of the English Dominican Province, pp. 10–13.

(3) Thomas Aquinas, *Summa contra Gentiles,* Bk. II, Ch. 38; same transl. p. 83. Cf. Bk. I, Ch. 8; p. 15.

(4) Thomas Aquinas, *Summa Theologica,* Pt. I, qu. 46, art. 2, Answer; same transl., p. 250.

(5) Thomas Aquinas, *Summa Theologica,* Pt. II^{a}–II^{ae}, qu. II, art. 4; pp. 36–37. *Summa contra Gentiles,* Bk. I, Ch. 4; pp. 7–9.

(6) Thomas Aquinas, *Summa Theologica,* Pt. II^{a}–II^{ae}, qu. I, art. 5, ad 3^{m}; p. 12. A complete exposition of Saint Thomas' position will be found in: *In Boetium de Trinitate,* qu. II, art. 3, Resp.; in *Opuscula omnia,* ed. P. Mandonnet, Vol. III, p. 51.

(7) As translated by Alb. Hyma, *The Imitation of Christ,* The Century Co., New York, 1927. In that edition, the second of the quoted texts will be found in Bk. III, Ch. 35, p. 139.

(8) P. Pourrat, *Christian Spirituality in the Middle Ages,* Burns Oates, London, 1924; Vol. II, pp. 253–256.

Cf. ALB. HYMA, *The Christian Renaissance: a History of the Devotio Moderna,* The Century Co., New York, 1925, and the Preface to the above-mentioned translation of *The Imitation of Christ,* pp. VII–XXXI.

(9) P. POURRAT, *op. cit.,* Vol. II, pp. 268–284.

(10) On that treatise, see M. WINDSTOSSER, *Étude sur la théologie germanique,* Paris, 1911.

(11) As translated in P. POURRAT, *op. cit.,* Vol. III, p. 78.

(12) See the remarkable essay of P. VIGNAUX, *Luther commentateur des sentences,* Paris, J. Vrin, 1935.

(13) M. LUTHER, *Disputatio contra scholasticam theologiam* (1517); Weimar edit., Vol. I, pp. 221–228. Cf. E. GILSON, *Le moyen âge et le naturalisme antique,* in *Archives d'histoire doctrinale et littéraire du moyen âge,* Vol. VII (1932), pp. 14–21.

(14) On the exact meaning of James' attitude towards the religious problem, see R. B. PERRY, *The Thought and Character of W. James;* Little, Brown and Co., Boston, 1935; Vol. I, pp. 164–166.

(15) H. BERGSON, *Les deux sources de la morale et de la religion,* Paris, F. Alcan, 1932; p. 256.

(16) R. OTTO, *The Idea of the Holy,* transl. by J. W. Harvey, Oxford Univ. Press, 4th edit., 1926, p. 182.

INDEX

OF NAMES

Index of Names

Abelard, 12
Albertus Magnus (Saint Albert the Great), 14–15, 60, 70
Alexander of Hales, 70
Anselm, Saint, 22–27, 31, 32, 75, 81, 87
Aristotle, 6, 9, 12, 17, 38–39, 53, 79, 80, 93–94
Augustine, Saint, 16–24, 32
Averroes, 38–55, 58, 60, 64–66, 79–80, 84, 87
Avicenna, 38–39

Bacon, Francis, 95
Bacon, Roger, 28–30
Bergson, 96–98
Bernard, Saint, 12–13
Boethius of Dacia, 59, 65
Bonaventura, Saint, 22, 70

Cajetan, 84–85
Cano, M., 95
Clement of Alexandria, 16

Damiani, Saint Peter, 13
Dante, 60
Descartes, R., 95
Duns Scotus, 85–87, 90

Eckhart, Meister, 90
Epicureans, the, 6, 12, 17
Erasmus, Desiderius, 91–92, 94

Fontenelle, 65

Galileo, 37
Gaunilo, 25
Gazali, 39
Gerson, John, 90–91
Gioberti, 22
Groote, Gerhard (Groot, Gerritt), 90

Huesden, John Vos de, 91

James, William, 96–97
John of Jaudun, 61–63
John of Saint Thomas, 84
John, Saint, 16, 23
Justin Martyr, 16

Lull, Ramon, 30–31
Luther, Martin, 92–94

Maimonides, Moses, 69
Malebranche, 22, 32
Maritain, Jacques, 84

Marsiglio di Padoa, 61
Mohammed, 38, 52
Moses, 52

Origen, 16
Otto, Rudolf, 98

Paul, Saint, 7, 9–10, 15–16
Perry, R. B., 96
Petrarch, 92
Plato, 6, 12, 17, 20, 22, 23, 24
Plotinus, 20, 22, 23, 24, 38

Ruysbroeck, John, 90

Siger of Brabant, 59–60, 65, 81
Socrates, 17
Stoics, the, 6, 12, 17

Tatian, 11–12
Tempier, Etienne, 64
Tertullian, 8–10, 12
Thomas à Kempis, 91
Thomas, Saint, 22–23, 60, 66–85, 90, 95, 99
Todo, Jacopone da, 13–14

Valentius, 9
Vitoria, Fr. de, 95
Voltaire, 63

William of Ockham, 86–87, 90